Collected Poems

JOHN CHUBACK

Cover art Conformity (front) and Courage (back) copyright October 2020.
Oil Stick on paper.

By John A Chuback

ISBN: 9-798-7409812-1-5

Table of Contents

iv

The Fate of a Seed
We Planted

The voyages of all mankind combined could never find
A man whose pen does spill like this when you are in his mind.
You are art, alive with breath, you make the words arise
I write and sketch and sculpt and paint but can't express your eyes.

With a face so perfect, beauty's hand is yours
The cheetah streaks by sprinting, and the lions unleash roars.
My, world, my jungle, cannot rest
Until my head lies on your breast.

Don't overlook what must be seen
Your body curves, so smooth, so lean
That I am yours and if you left
Then all Earth's lovers are bereft.

Don't try to fool yourself with thought
That somewhere love like this is bought.
And realize dear that is not so
A love like ours needs tears to grow.

We sewed the seed so long ago
So, to the wind you must not throw
This life which we've begun to make
Do not commit this one mistake.

Make errors any other place
But you should not our love disgrace.
Have pride in what love we have shared
No man has ever this much cared.

I write for you and hope you read
I trust within you have some need
To have me standing at your side
And turn to me your eyes with pride.

The wreckage of a vessel washed to shore

Will you ever look at me the way I do at you?
Why when we were happy, did this result ensue?
A body carved in marble and cast in precious ore
You and your friends sneer at me and poke me 'til I'm sore.

I remember days when you were proud that I was yours
Before your many boatsmen started tugging on the oars.
Away you drifted, quick not slow
From river's bank I shout, "please no!"

But you don't care about me, I guess you never did
I should have known you'd do this, but in your trap I slid.
The hope is still within me, growing there each day
I pray you reconsider or the offer goes away.

To waste true love like we still share is tragedy indeed
I remember when you did, so I too with you will plead.
You are so shortsighted, you always need good times
Out I squeeze my twisted guts fighting with these rhymes.

I took you from the dungeon, and gave you all I could
My family and myself and friend, it simply did no good.
You had to start to do again what you had done before
You run with scum and failures, it's they that you adore.

It will scratch at you
once you have
pet it enough

Even while you love me not
I think of your kind eyes.
You walk and sit and move with rot
Forget the ancient lies.

Through the skies you have to soar
Like the marlin has to leap
You are in me at my core
The price they charge is steep.

Know the leopard you see run
His spots are hard to read.
Once he's eaten, he is done
So never let him feed.

Trust me I was big cat once
It's hard to take I know
But know that I've been made the dunce
You all must think I'm slow.

Know that I write from the blood
My father gave to me
I try to pull you from the flood.
Do know you can be free.

I'm not ashamed to love you
I'm proud that you're my pride,
Tell me now, what I can do,
These words are born inside.

Things Around the House

I lie here like a Persian rug
And you just lie, and lie, and lie.
You stand, and step, and walk on me
I hide my eyes and cry.

I lie here like a porcelain lamp
And you just lie, and lie, and lie.
I shine but you don't see my light
I hide my face and cry.

I sit here like a crystal vase
And you just lie, and lie, and lie.
Each sparkle gets its life from you
I drop my head and cry.

I sit here like a rocking chair
And you just lie, and lie, and lie.
You force me back as I come up
I turn away and cry.

But you don't think I cry for you
You don't think that I cry.
You are my love and yes, I do
But they all ask me why.

I do not shed these tears
Without great pain you see
Because of what has happened
I feel I am not me.

I see you with some other
And cry in rage and hurt.
I see you smile at me
I fall and clutch your skirt.

Time Line: Pi r Squared

I

Why can't I be the only one who wrote what I have
written?

II

Do men have faded scars in spots where little
boys get bitten?

III

Does a little girl think naughty things and a
woman skip by pig-tailed?

IV

Does a boy of five need fast red cars because
his daddy's wig failed?

A Poem Exposing the Educated Moron

What is the *Philosofor*
I ponder passing through the door.
What is it that he really seeks,
While from his mouth the feces leaks?

"Shut up, you stupid fuck," I say!
"Take your books and get away."
Your talk leads nowhere, Dr. Want,
I scream out, "Stop," but you just Kant.

Now seated in the lecture hall,
I start to cringe; you have a ball.
Why won't this coward just conclude?
"Fuck you! I'm sorry, that was rude."

We all have questions come to us
But from our mouths we don't squirt pus.
Admit you haven't figured out
What all this shit is all about.

And while you read from Socrates,
The boredom brings me to my knees.
Walking out I zip my pack
And drop my essay on the stack.

Read All About It!

Standing at the bus stop.
I wait.

A man walks his dog.
It barks.

He yawns.

Rolling his eyes,
He puts his ass close to the ground
And shits on the curb.

I open the paper
Unphased by the stink of the fresh crap.

Jotting Data in
His Personal Journal

I imagine,

For the first
Time...

A mouse runs scrambly by
The lab bench,
And I stick
A wad
Of typewriter paper
Paper
Lousy paper
Sheets
And sheets of it.
Up his little asshole! Butt!
You like a flower shop's
Fragrance,
The methanol helps
Because they cannot
Avoid the guillotine,
The rats.
Rats rats rats rats
You will be
Surprised and actually quite comfortable.
And trust and
Be overwhelmed comfortably

By Me.

Having Received A Red Envelope
(13 February 1992)

A surprise in the shape of red envelope

Sat still, near his pile of books that night. Tearing the seal, tempted hands dance with hope;

And, brown eyes leap inside to see say what it might.

Then a word, and a phrase, and a line--

Like a sun shower's unforeseen gift.

In a bed of down feathers, she force his recline;

More finely than flour her penned-thoughts he sift.

She omitted that word has no meaning:

Most ubiquitous slang slung with slime.

Now, from his head-heart careening

Comes the ever-omit, and ink-emote rhyme.

How cherished he her love card, his sonnet could not express.

Unbuttoning hands they will tell her, as they unwrap the valentine
    dress.

Summer

You have seen
Yourself
For the first time

Short woolen pile
Beneath
Our quiet afternoon

Persian carpet
Woven
So complexly

Mirrored doors
Angled
To reflect embrace

Pearl

A grain of sand hardly at all,
I tumble and roll through the waves.
I gasp for a chance at breath, only to choke.
You, the hard-shelled oyster,
Spread the valves and bear your slippery inside to me.
Resting in a tiny pocket of bubbles,
I hope to escape but the shell slams shut about me,
Forcing most of the sea outside.
Caught within, at first I am panicked, like falling in love.
You hold me, I am safe,
And I change because of what I am and what you are.
I realize as the sea throws us,
That we are now something together.
You don't trap me inside,
I do not poison your shimmering body.
Together we grow,
We leave your shell to the foamy salt.
A shiny, slick skinned pearl,
Whole and full,
We emerge.

A Play About Players
Who Are Always Acting
But Might Otherwise Be
Good Friends of Mine

Walking along the foot of the stage from out of the wings appear two young men. The background is cut off by a black curtain which falls about mid-stage.

ME:

> There's nothing like visiting old friends at Christmas time.
>
> It's a great reminder of who your old friends are.
>
> I'm always amazed, no matter how well I try to prepare myself, at how little of them I can tolerate.
>
> They're always so very intoxicated.

Now the curtain comes up slowly, but with no warning. We are walking toward their table at the club Christmas party.

THEM:

> Now Shon, what kind of a coat is that?
>
> Lose the belt!
>
> How 'bout a beer?
>
> Where did you get it dear, the Salvation Army?
>
> (The whole gang busts out chuckling whitely, while the one who always drinks the most describes us to a stranger as an Arab and an Israeli.)
>
> Soliloquizing under a white spotlight, with them, still amused, sitting in silent silhouette.

SHON (ME):

> You wouldn't recognize a Salvation Army store if I stuck the whole building in your sun-dried ass
>
> Hole in a rich man's bed!
>
> You don't know me.

But I lived with you, visiting at times like this.

If only I could treat this old feeling of nausea and still drive home.

And they continue as if I'm enjoying it along with them.

A conversation strikes up.

Shon:

(Responding to voice-less players):

No brie for me thanks, I've already made a true hog of myself.

Oh, so things are fine with Doug in the far east, that's good.

Hey, fine!

That's wonderful!

Great!

Oh yeah? hum? wow! well! O.K.!

They ask for more wine and then whine about the quality of the wine they whined for. The fat one breaks wind thunderously, Zeus gone mad, but she is adored by them all so no one comments about how rude she is. Shon shows a sour expression of displeasure as the sickening smell of the place finally reaches his side of the table.

(TECHNICAL DIRECTION:

An unceasing, winding tone created by a violin is substituted for their silence as their mouths continue to jaw furiously.)

And they continue as if I'm enjoying it along with them.

Exiting through the rear of the stage, Shon and the towering ghost.

I trade a lusty glance with the thick legged red-head who I've known.

She smirks coyly.

If only I had treated this old feeling of nausea, we could have gotten into a taxi (Says the sidekick catching the exchange.)

And they continue as if I'm enjoying it along with them.

The captain enters after we leave to say the bar is closed. A nasty fist fight breaks out in the room. They fight for what they believe in.

Fade lighting to black.

Drop black curtain mid stage.

All encores done upstage of black curtain.

Who? This Guy Here?
For the Birds.

Big eyes
And a big beak.
Ni   ght   an
d t   h   e   o   wl
is   not   near
asleep in that big
dark tree.
Looking for a fat rat.
A boy "WHOO" knows the way of
the birds looks up to the owl atop
the stark, leafless monument of pure
nature. No one understands this "BOY!"
and his fascination with the stealth-like
predatory creatures of keen-sighted blood
thirsty-ness. They stalk their prey in
dissimilar fashion--one uses surgical
sharpness of talon--one uses a ZOOM
lens and night-defiant flash cube.
I may understand him a bit. Whoo
cares is not his greatest pre
occupation

So We

Endure...
Privately together—
The drought;

On soil:
Never tested by seed.
The sun

Splashes
Blue pails of cool water.
Enraged

I put
Calloused hands 'round sickle,
And plow

As if
I myself were the ox!
Always

I see
Growing on the field's edge—
Far off,

A row
Of proud corn stalks: yellow,
Stretching

Their backs
And arms, not needing rest.
Narrow

Signs of
How the hot sweat smells of
Sweet corn.

Sunlight
Slips through the tall green leaves
To me.

I roll
In the scorching, loose dirt;
Thinking

Of how
Worthwhile white rain would make
Chapped smiles.

Dining Without Reservation

Toothless butterknife
Presses down
The glazed skin
Of the square
Cheese danish
Until
The spot below the metal
Is so dense, and thin,
That the whole length of blade
Disappears and only
The handle, with my finger
Along the top edge shows.
Then, a bit more force
Snaps the compressed pastry
And this happens again and then
More regularly--
Indicated by a series of clicks
Against the diner's breakfast plate.
A dish of greasy-over-easies
Sweep below my chin
And crash in front of the chum
Next to me.
The waitress mumbles
Something about enjoying it.
I notice
That the sign on the door
Says that
The rest of the world is sorry
But it is closed to us.
He has his eggs.
I have my danish.

The Farm

Mountain flowers from the wood line.
Sunday morning along the tractor path.
Crisp air entices yet green leaves.

The view inspires me to tell my lover.
The corn on the adjacent rise--
Defining the roads edge like tightly packed cilia.

Tested over and over, she and I.
A glimpse of the rooftop and the carriage-house.
The doctor dissects the field.

She held them for an hour, she said.
I hold her attention
A flower, bouquet, is not the mountain.

Thunderstorm

Outside of the glass apartment,
      the electrical storm cracks black night.

An enraged sky shatters into
      a thousand grains of brightly burning molten ash.

It settles lightly on the tormented
      throws of the invisible cold ocean.

I listen to thunder split silence
      arrhythmically...

Constantly catching the never-readied ear
      a second too early.

A heaviness, a labored-ness to my breathing
      brings me back to our walk

Of yesterday afternoon, slalom-like
      along the splintery wooden boards.

How I felt a little dizzy out there
      in the "good sun" you told me about.

I walked in the snowstorm for the tire
      I dreamt about two nights ago

Because you held my hand on returning
      from the counter service pizza shop.

Each time I kiss you as we sleep,
        it is to tell you everything I am telling,

Haven't told, want to tell--
        everything you will come to know as me.

On a Cold Autumn Day

Calm, silent, frozen winter streams back.
Limb-launched whirly-bird sits in sidewalk crack.
The crinkly mosaic, musty--bunkers our street;
Shuffle, shuffle--curbside three o'clock retreat.
Orange-lined green parka, stitched through and through.
Gray fake-fur rims hoods, smiling mouth grape-blue.
Quiet, gentle, snow-skinned girl curls warmly--
Stiff vibrant carrot protrudes informally.
Cold man winter puts heat in the house--
Stirring, stirring, especially the mouse.

Truth

Blue-orange-red-night sky-- the eve
Of someday, a day away.
The sky she will have,
With a Pollack proud spray of stars sparkling.
The bright, dark dirt-road, clean-white-light moon.
The mouth of the creek, the moths on the porch-door-- illuminated!
Childish fear of the darkness...mine and hers.
Two twos, or even four, yet, your only tools-- beside you.
And, what I have to tell you.
Childhood, gingerbread, snow storm, snow day, sleigh-ride dreams.
Live young woman
True.

Old Man

I want to be an old man now,
With hair as white as bone--
With a patchwork of amoeboid liver-spots
All over my sunken cheeks and inflamed knuckles.
I want to sit anyplace and just be placid--
Too wise at last, too experienced to raise a fist,
To the differentiation and division
That continues to evolve...metaplastically.
Simply, sit and think about women I had held
And, the one who finally mattered.
I want to meet young people though--
Introduce myself, hopeful and unfearful.
To see if we could talk.
I want my flesh to be fluid,
Seep around my bones, And flow over the mattress fully.
Awaiting by then, only the next morning--perhaps.
I want a cane—
Just so I can walk,
And not to be a widower.
I want to love this woman forever.
I want to be very quiet,
Softly speaking only when truly necessary.
I want her always to love me.
Our children, and theirs would care for us--
Feel no shame in our company—
Nor burden.
I shall earn, I hope, their respect,
As my mother and father have so many times again earned mine.
I want to wear a hat,

More old than I am now, by far--
And comb my hair very neatly
Early each morning--
Slowly, in front of a full-length beveled-mirror.
I'll buy a newspaper every morning
And read on the porch of the public library
For an hour, with my wife.

The Bosom

Silken slips of even breath
Through evening nostrils pass.
Our poem-dance does put to death
All history's once known las.
She resting now cheek pillow pressed
My fingertips explore;
I sleep within the bosom-nest
And, feel for nothing more.

Trust and Truth

Walk silently along my side
At sea, or in our mountains.
Lead the way, my thoughtful guide
To drink of streaming fountains.
Stray not from each other let's;
And, leap from shore to landing.
Contentment trust and truth begets--
Neglect not understanding.
Come, come and show me
Free of word, your innermost emotion
And I will let you also see
Another undived ocean.

Bumble Bee

A bumble bee comes zipping around,
whipping around, chasing the kitten's tail
in shifting orbits, creating the doppler
around my head.

His fat belly, yellow and black,
striped like a miniature tiger,
bumps into the chubby lobe
of my ear.

Bumble bee legs hang packed
with pollen, and dangle forward
and back each time his stomach knocks
the side of my head.

His buzzing is endless, relentless,
and louder and softer as he goes
far and comes near from the ledge
in my ear.

I won't let him sit there,
I won't let him rest there,
let him go elsewhere to rant
than my ear.

What is it he's saying
that is so important, that
he wants me knowing, and shouts
at my ear?

If he would sit nicely
where he could not sting me,
then maybe I'd listen, but
now he's too near.

I fear for my ear lobe,
that this fellow pierce it,
and leave it disfigured, and all
at what end?

Away pesky fellow, and stop
manic flying, around my head;
looping, you've said what
you've said.

Your voice tells me nothing,
you've got my arms flailing,
I'm running to nowhere, to flee
from your dread.

My heart is now pounding
so hard I hear nothing,
I sprint for the river to bury
my head.

Down I come crashing, and
on the bank splashing
the water up at you, and soak
myself wet.

And still, you keep spinning
about my skull quickly,
and holler your message, that I
can't make out.

My face is now dripping
with water I've splashed there,
but yet my mouth's parched from the
fear that I feel.

I dunk my head fully,
into the water, and hoping you'll
vanish, I strain to
see where.

I still hold my breath,
relieved yet at nothing,
'cause though I can't hear you, you
still may be there.

Too soon it's apparent
the choice that I'm left with,
to face you and listen, or stay
without air.

Exhausted and breathless,
I come up with fury,
bee-beaten, in-screaming a huge
mouth of air.

Down on my back with my
hair squashed in mud,
my eyes both tear-flooded, you zip
past my face.

In my small finger, my flesh
is of muscle, surpassing
most greatly the weight
of your whole.

Yet, having not touched me,
I like a pig, am rolling in
puddles and squealing
with fear.

My throat quick-collapsing,
I search for your body
that carries the stinger I guess
will appear.

And suddenly Bumble resorts to
more humble behavior, and sits
in still silence atop
my nose bridge.

Slamming my eyelids, I
cringe fully thinking
that now that he's dropped me,
he'll puncture my face.

Awaiting the punishing mark
of defeat, I soon
become shocked that he still
hasn't stung me.

Relaxing my wrinkled,
spasmodic expression, I let
my eyes open to see where
he's gone.

My eyes open wider than
I had expected, for I
found it shocking he yet
topped my nose.

Now slowly he walked, as my
chest regained normal,
and less panicked rhythms, and
fear went away.

Then little footsteps tickled
my cheek, as the bumble bee,
buzzless, made fast toward
my ear.

Dry mud crumbled as I bent
my knuckles white, and the
bee stopped his stepping at the
bluff of my ear.

"Don't take the frightful
noise my wings beat,
for my voice giant creature," he gently
sang down.

Laundry Day

Soon I
Find
Room in my heart

For another.
And
Unlike her

I don't bother
With
Feeling forever.

Renting whatever
Rooms
Remain vacant.

So onward I
Go
Wishing only

That washing
The
Clothes was worth doing.

Elegy of Hope-Romance

Black streamers
At
The funeral home-

Unnecessary death
Of
The hope-romance.

Rivers winding
And
Finding their way-

Reflecting pools
Have
Fools faces shimmer.

Linoleum flooring
As
The adoring basin.

Hope-children crying,
And
Dying is hope-romance.

An undeveloped Composition

Snapshots never taken-
Never better than
Finger-faded photographs.

At the lake house-
Always time for
Tadpole dreams on rafts

Ripples run out one way
Then back again,
Unboxing ribboned hats.

Flowers hug the drain-ditch.
Then through empty pages
Of the should-have-album do we pass.

And Will We Meet Again?

"Bye", said she
And
Sadly, "Wait", said I.

But it was
Too
Late by this time.

Next--Nothing
Left.
No words would

Be heard.
And
I hung it up at last.

Calling back
Could
Do no good

It seemed.
Yet,
I dreamed, and I did.

To rid ourselves
Of
Empty shelves.

Laundry Lines

Quiet--No static
On
Our wash-line.

Listening, pained
By
Sputtering autumn creeks.

Down a mile
The
Lush apple orchard.

Brown leaves crinkle
In
September's silence.

Both Spider's Webs and Flakes of Snow

Both spiders' webs and flakes of snow
Of streetcleaners will live past this sonnet's days.
You too my love will have to go
In all the different ways.
When the sun's warm rays melt the drifts,
And a zephyr ruins the widow's home,
You'll be gone despite these gifts-
Rolled off in a long black Brougham.
Like the ink, you shall run dry;
And in a box, you're bound to fade.
But not because I did not try,
I even write this in the shade!
That you'll be dead you best be sure,
For no disease these lines can cure.

Ah, To Know the Moon
Is There

It really is the way you look at things--
Like the moon for one.
At least a billion or more miles
Away from here,
But yet I can see it
Very plainly like everyone else.
And I do not believe
That there is anything
Unusual
About feeling sure
That each night,
If it is clear,
The moon will be there
For me to look at
And wonder about.
What difference would it make
If I could stand on its surface?
Other than not being able to fully
Appreciate it?
Only seeing a tiny bit.
To the horizon
No matter how far
I walk.
It looks so flat from there I'm sure.
Like here if one is here
I suppose,
It would never appear

So round and full,
Bright and unbridled,
From right next to it.
I bet Armstrong would never
Even know
How far off in space he was
If he were born there, or something.
You have to be far away-
To fill your eyes with the whole thing.
So, when you get there,
You will truly see
The beauty,
And the roundness.

Ballet Without Pomp

Most beautiful for that moment.
In a hanging pair of men's knee pants!
She tucks a ribbon of hair,
Like a strand of faded, yellow, Chinese silk,
Elegantly behind her ear.
She presses upward—toes undressed,
Delicate and perfect
Like an early spring.
Her strong calves take a deep breath.
Turning bashfully, she sees
I find her charming.
I watch her dance effortlessly.
I cheer from the entrance to the kitchen.
I am her only audience.
Inside I feel like ten thousand people
Devouring the performance
At her feet
As they stand.
I cross my arms around her back.
Hoping she will know...
That I have seen the Bolshoi

Othello, Envy My Desdemona

I and she the spider do make.
So carefully balanced we crawl.
Moving barely, behind her, her breath I do take,
And by moonlight: a shadow cast huge on the wall.
Lying flat, breathing slow,
With her lips to my cheek;
Pressing hard do we flow
As her name I do speak.
And she feels deep within
Lying still, on the floor,
A web we do spin
With our limbs twice of four.
But creating arachnids requires a knack,
There is more to this creature than belly to back.

E. Fruit

The peach:
My plum,

Sits so -- Ripe,
So delicious.

Strong rooted
Teeth.
Bite daringly!

Indulgent succulence
Running down

From palm
To elbow
(Along the forearm).

On the First Floor Landing

The scoundrel
    slid down the
        banister and
            drowned *Whisk,*
                his kitten,
                    in the same
                        saucer of
                            once still
                                white milk.

Unresolution

So senseless—
This
Silent existence.

The violence
Via
Sans-satellite.

Immaturity marks
The
New immensities

Making sure
That
She remains shielded.

Unhealed
By
Her absence.

Discontented during
The
Disappearance of discourse.

Why I Swam to the
Bottom of the Lake

Coming to the edge of a lake
Which I always bathed in and skipped stones on,
I grabbed a perfectly round
pebble from the muddy shore.
It was half stuck
But I wiggled my finger under one edge
to get it loosened a little,
And then I thought the fight was over.
A very strange thing happened though,
You see, I threw it almost straight upward,
(A very tight angle anyway)
And not a splash was made.
Nor a wave sent across
The water's glassy surface.
How strange I thought--
Palming another similar piece of stone
Up from the ground,
Again, I whistled it high through the air,
And down it came with a gastric
Kerplop!
And now,
My arm sore from throwing stones,
I have decided to get
The special one back.
And I won't test it.
I'm sure that the shore
Is not covered
With ones like that
One.

Bells

The telephone
And I:
Are presently
Involved...
In a standoff!

We are both
So quiet.
Only yesterday morning we were
So close to one another

Attrition

The telephone
And I:
Are presently
Involved...
In a standoff!

We are both
So quiet.
Only yesterday morning-
We were
Holding on with determination.

Inside A Tree

Tall, I cast shadow on all else.
This height I get from you
Water--rebirth.
An oak, or redwood.
Whatever I am,
I am enormous.
Within, your nectars, nutrients,
Fill each vein.
Unending is my strength
Knowing you are
At my roots.
Rushing elements
Vital to my power
Through the soil,
You lie beneath me perfectly.
Most sacred,
Most truthful,
The most
Beautiful song of bird
The wind has
Ever borne.
I lean
To drink
And secret essences of your perfumes
Course swiftly through me.
Like the fragrance of a hundred
Thousand saffron bits
You fill my lungs.
Wood so dead

So dark
Without you.
The night:
My sweet syrup,
Viscous and black,
Pouring out
Over the sea.

The Fire

Sitting by the fire
Red wine flows like a river in spring.

Sitting by the fire
Flames flicker in the darkness.

Sitting by the fire
Embers crackle in the silence.

Five Minutes

Five minutes
Here and there.

Five fleeting minutes
Here and there.

Measured by footsteps on the ancient wooden floor boards
Here and there.

Muffled voices in the twisted hallways of the old estate
Here and there.

Strewn about like ribbons of shredded poetry
Here and there.

Like the pendulum bob on a grandfather clock
Alternating endlessly to-and-fro –
Here... and... there

Marking time -
Forever... and... ever

A Poem About Down Primarily

Marrow-winds sneak into the woolen overcoat you wear.
And you think that it's better to
Look someplace else for warmth, rather than stand
Out here. All summer long it seems that that
Vulture has been gliding in tireless determination,
Elegantly and gracefully. At the edge of the
Lake, the fair skinned scout hooks a pretty little, four
Inch bluegill. First time for that seems
Especially important I would have to
Suppose, for a fellow like him. But, often the first
Catch will
Out-wriggle the inexperienced, undeserving
Novice. So, I was wrong about the
Catbird, perhaps; I did not know
Exactly the call it might make naturally
And, consequently was unable to know if it
Lied, or sang
Entirely as it would if a tree fell with only the
Dogs to say what they had heard.
All the time the colors had been changing in
The trees, and I had been watching.
The leaves appeared as green to me as they
Had when first I went into the woods. How I
Ever missed noticing I don't yet know.
Proof that
Every bluegill may be the same. It's not
Right to say, but, still I must
Insist that until I felt this

Persistent wind, and began to see winter, I
Had no idea that the hot sun could vanish so
Entirely--Just like that!
Really, it's very alarming to think this time of
Year has already arrived.

Interior Design
(Modified Sonnet Sequence)

The formidable prospect of tearing down and re
placing the existing wallpaper in this square
looking old room. And the many layers of pain
t which lay below—so stealth, so clandestine.
Those out-of-style, out-with-the-flood colors,
their many planes of antiquity, and cigarette
soot-stained faces--the faces of coal-miners,
a breed so diminished. Coat over coat in flat
sheets, always at one time all was so perfect.
Taking a scraper from the canvas drop cloth, I
remember birthday parties where everyone would
be given a gigantic jawbreaker, the concentric
spheres of hard candy--too big at first to fit
in your mouth all at once, and your tongue the

News report being received almost
immediately after the various
strata of this world had been uncovered.
                              Patches of torn paper
                  left sticking to the last
            generation of paint. Light
            gray: fashion--
            able
even now
                              And a pungent rasp
berry
from when this had been
            my oldest sister's bedroom.
To have chosen that shade!

But now she lives somewhere else.
Hard work--
        removing old wall paper.

                I doubt it will need
                wetting though. That job

won't be necessary
here. Just takes
        pealing,
        scraping,
            and
              tear-
                ing.

Only

                              very

                stubborn

        patches

                        left

                at

spots

here

and

up

here

Paint
 ing t
  hese
   old w
    alls
     won't
      be to
       o bad
        I don
         't th
          ink.
           Rolls
            on so
             easy.

In fl
at cl
ean s
woosh
es wh
ich c
ling
to th
e pla
ster--
board
so wa
nting
ly.

No bristly, scratchy
  brushes when I put it
    on. Only aluminum pa
     ns filled with creamy
       latex—something that
      a child would like to dr
     ink with a white straw and
red stripe down the middle of it.
A set-up like that--along with some
new rollers and spongy cylindrical pads
to fit them with for each new coat. And fina
lly, when the labour has been exacted of me, i
t will most certainly begin to be replaced as
I near the end. I will re-meet satisfactions.

Like the evening undergoing surgery, I remove
myself from the perimeter of the room for a n
ew perspective. The fumes enhance my sense o
f accomplishment somewhat, but the windows ha
ve been open just enough so that I am sure th
at the work is truly very competent. Desire
of the future has helped to create this reviv
ed place to spend lonely nights, or share pas
sionate ones with strong legged women. And f
eeling finished at last, I sit with the spott
ed dropcloth and begin to wait quietly, when
suddenly I notice that one spot in the corner
, beneath the window sill has somehow remains
d completely unrevised and as it was.

Tuesday

Tuesday comes and I sit alone
At the dock awaiting your arrival.

I wonder where you are -
Most likely at the bus stop.

I pray today will be a better day,
With more time for love.

I quietly thank God once again
for bringing you back into my life.

I look at my wristwatch and hope
That I'll hear your laugh,

Like a symphony down the pier,
By the time I cast my first net

Sonnet

A world we live in like the breeze
We know not our next turn.
A glass of wine, a bread, a cheese --
Another book to learn.
I break an egg to make a meal
But yet I split the shell.
One cannot fix what cannot heal --
A fish left out will smell.
The food we use, and take from it
The nutrients it holds.
Like the piglet on the tit
One loses face in the folds.
And in a world where wind blows not,
One clears his nose of viscous snot.

Firdausi

Sixty-thousand couplets Firdausi did create.
The coins of gold from Mahmud arrived in Tus too late.
And now as I write number two,
I promise more than gold to you.
And now a thousand years gone by,
I'm sure I can't but still I try
To give too you Just twenty lines
And, with the ore, send sweet red wines.
So maybe you can feel it too,
The drunkenness I get from you.
The finest fabrics brought by ship
To match the pinkness of your lip.
And gowns, and blouses will be sewn--
A woman that no poet's known!
I come by land and you by air,
For a "second-ary" stare.
And I, the artist, stand and see
What man does dare compete with me;
So small with nothing you can use,
I let him play but make him lose.
So sad that I had not known then
This better place to put my pen.
So when this futile contest ends
We go which way the river wends;
And then when I am sure at last
I will into the water cast
A bate that you will not swim past--
Or choose to for your whole life fast.

Farming

If the rain were to stop right now,
Tomorrow the fields we'd plow.
But if the rain doesn't stop today,
It will wash all the seeds away--
Or drown the crop to come--
Or we drown ourselves in rum.

To survive the rain must stop!

Or ruin the yearly crop...
And the old cow so obese--
And the black clouds will not cease,
And I wonder where the sun is,
Or whether the harvest is his.

I remember the grain standing high!

In a pile of hay, we would lie...
A thousand acres of beans--
In my white flannel shirt and my jeans.
But the sky was bright blue
And I always had you.

But now in the day the sky's black!

And I cannot see if your back...
The wind says that Mother Earth's mad--
I think back to blue times that we had.
Then no farmer could reap like I did,

Or raise at the auction my bid.
But one has come along
And he's ruined my song.

He has somehow developed a seed!

It is never affected by weed...
And the water it takes--
So, for both of our sakes
I ask you if you've gotten home.
The river swirls sickly with foam.

Where we use to swim!

And jump from the limb...
Of the giant old oak--
Blistered hands and feet I soak.

THE POLLUTION IS MAKING ME SICK!

When the rain had stopped,
Off a turkey's head we lopped.
And feast replaced the storm.
A field of view began to form
Which let me see the harm
That might have made the farm
A dream, like she had said--
Scattering pig slop by the shed
I saw white clouds sweep,
And in the pond a bullfrog leap
A sure sign we succeeded.

"That rain is what we needed"!

I said with great conviction...
Full knowing it was fiction--
I myself did wonder
If time would end with thunder
That roared about the land.
But now I kept her hand,
And things were fine for good.
And in a week, there stood
Just inches from the earth,
A sign of our new birth;

A tiny sprig of spring!

I knew what it would bring...
A full-grown stalk for reaping--
The catbird flew by peeping.
I found that moment so absurd.
How was it that I knew
Her song was so untrue?
And hardly seeing her,
She flew by in a blur.

No one heard her call.

Making Poetry

The thick sticky ink
Fills up the shaft.
Inside her I sink
The poem (my craft):
Changing the roll
Of the tip up and down.
I'm in it now whole
And stain not her gown.
Each poem we write,
I always have more;
Deep into the night,
Into it I pour.
And always our couplet enhances eve's end--
Together with arched neck and back do we bend.

Invention

The moon did seem so far away
From Earth at one time, when
Tractors and road cars ran on hay-
And dreams were small of men.
Then two stood up like very few;
At Kittyhawk, we saw what was Wright.
And then for space they chose a crew,
Though Einstein said no speed of light!
Can mankind prove a genius wrong;
With heart, and not with logic?
And though the distance was quite long,
The end might have been tragic.
So never be impatient or sleep without a dream,
Time is passing quickly although slow it may seem.

The Wonderful Absurdity of Consciousness

Dreaming of a dream, she said
That probably my plans are
Color pictures in my head.
Perhaps indeed they are fetched far.
But yet, for slumber it is real.
For now, I can enjoy.
On a tray is spread a meal
Of creamy peas, there sits a boy.
A cry from baby in the dream,
But she knows what he needs.
Although outrageous it does seem,
From her breast our child feeds.
Absurdity wakes me and proves it's untrue-
The wife is yet one, while the children are two.

Garden Overgrowing

Oh! Poor sapling growing here.
Should I uproot you totally?
I know it would appear
It would end-up unfruitfully,
The soil was not rich,
Though water I have given;
Maybe I should switch
To a species which has thriven
In my garden in the past.
Forget about this sapling--
Prune another, make it last.
Although, this one is darling.
I know if I clear all my land.
For me she'll blossom grown in sand.

Compare not the words

I read William's of this form
They said his hand was deft.
But even not the fiercest storm
Has ended leaving nothing left.
Always words can be applied
To feelings which are old,
Clouds roll out, skies open wide,
And like my will, the sun is bold.
If ever once I wanted one to
Read a poem that I wrote,
I would choose this, born of you--
And such would be the learned vote.
Perhaps my hand can't like his show it,
Still - you surpass she of that poet.

Apprentice

When last we parted, in a dream three artists did appear.
How to have you close when far, these gentlemen made clear

I wrote Van Gogh to him I said,
"I'd like a portrait made."
He came in on a starry night to see the plans were laid.
I told him that I wanted
To see what I missed so,
Not just angelic features,
But from within--her glow.
I said, "Dear Vincent do you think that you could get this
    done?"
He laughed and said, "The greatest thief can't steal from sky the
    sun!"
He handed me an address and told me I should go,
To him who taps in heartbeats,
Michelangelo.
I stuffed a sack and travelled to have him make from stone
an image of this woman without whom I'm alone.
He said his hands held talent,
They'd chisel me her face,
But told me that the thing I missed no sculpture could replace.
"An artist knows the boundaries,"
The sculptor said to me,
"Underneath the soil too, grows a leafless, rooted tree."
He gave to me a street name,
No number did appear.
He said that I should go there and shout the name Shakespeare.
I did just as he told me,

And flew there like the wren.
I asked the sonnet's master, "Sir would you be my pen?"
He scolded my arrival and said that I did lack.
He said they tried to tell me too,
The earless and hunchback.
He shouted from the window to the street where still I stood,
That he would not write you for me, for
In fame to search would do no good.
He threw to me a paper, and a long thin quill,
He told me reputation can never conquer will.
He sent me to my desk at home,
My journey ended there.
I write of the young woman,
Whose manner is most fair.

On a Trip Out to the Country

Two
Black cows-
Spotted white,
Stand at the dark,
Trampled edge,
And soak
Dry
Muzzles
Staring up
At the highway,
While my car
Follows
The
Solid
Yellow line
Of the black road.

From the Lakebed

Coming to the edge of a lake
Which I had always bathed in, and skipped stones on,
I grabbed a perfectly round
Pebble from the muddy shore.
It was half stuck
But I wiggled my finger under one edge
To get it loosened a little,
And then I thought the fight was over.
A very strange thing happened next-
You see I threw it almost straight upward,
(A very tight angle anyway)
And not a splash was made.
Nor a wave sent across
The water's glassy surface.
How strange I thought--
Palming another similar piece of stone
From the ground.
Again, I whistled it high through the air,
And down it came with a gastric
Splash.
And now,
My arm sore from throwing stones,
I have decided to get
The special one back.
And I won't test it.
I'm sure that the shore
Is not covered
With ones like that
one.

The Puppeteer

Four well crafted marionettes
Propped side by side on the metal shelf
Sit upright against the cool dimly shadowed wall
Awaiting the puppeteer in his quiet workshop

Each possessing perfectly tied square knots
At their wrists, elbows, hips and knees
And silky lengths of white twine
Fastened to a wooden cross-shaped handle

He carefully carved the marionettes by hand
The details were his passion
Every moment was either with or for them
And he missed them when he could not be there

But every evening when he returned
From the long hours of serious labor
The lights came on and joyful music perfumed the air
The puppet show began

He embraced each of their gifts
He had them dance and laugh and play
He controlled their movements with precision
Not a twitch was left to chance

They loved to make him happy
The olive-skinned man
He always had a sparkle in his eye and a pleasant smile on his lips
They came to life when he was around

He showed them all that they could do
Feats they felt were beyond their ability
He moved them about so effortlessly
With only a subtle tilt of his wrist this way or that

Then one by one when he knew the time had come
And after many years of constant instruction
He carefully untied the knots
Which had harnessed the marionettes

And see, none of them fell down flat
Although they were a bit clumsy at first
So unsure in their movements
Less graceful than when he had held the strings

And now they could go whichever way they wanted
Yes, they tried some new maneuvers
They explored some novel directions
But all felt most natural with the puppeteer's style in the end

Oh, and the creases of his smile became a little deeper
The vessels in his hands a little more pronounced
But the marionettes loved him more than ever
As he finally sat down and watched them perform

And over the years one by one
They brought him their own creations
Exquisite new figurines whom only he could show the way
And so, he gently picked up his supportive strings once more

And now they watch him display again his untarnished talent
As he helps them crawl and walk and talk
His uniquely infinite patience constantly sets the pace
And his boundless unconditional love is ever present

And they will always be safe with the puppeteer
Because in his hands lies the experience
Which will keep this magnificent show going
And now we all impatiently await his arrival in the otherwise cold
workshop

50 Years of This Sweet Life

It is morning once again.

18,250 beautiful mornings, never without her.

He sits at the kitchen table, soulfully singing an ancient Persian love song.

Sadi, Hafez, Rudaki... he knows them all by heart since childhood.

His mind still razor-sharp, like the scalpel blade he knew so well.

The tone of his voice still full and perfectly on pitch.

Golden sunlight spills in through the doorway from the dining room.

83 year-old hands, looking like those of a younger man, methodically pour the
glass of steaming red tea back and forth from the saucer, in rhythm with his tune.

Yes, this helps it cool... but it's the challenge that he loves.

It's a game. Even now, he plays like a child.

A cube of white sugar sits solidly between his teeth in anticipation of this sweet
life.

She stands at the sink with her left side and back to him.

He sees her in silhouette, washing the dishes and glancing out the window into
the neighbor's yard.

He finds her so beautiful.

So many wonderful days have started, just like this.

With new knees she stands stronger, taller and straighter than ever before...
defying time.

She is tireless, after so many years of hard work.

Putting the last dish in the drain-board to dry, she picks up half an orange that
one of the grandchildren left on the counter yesterday.

The once glistening surface, now a bit desiccated.

She is not deterred.

Hands still dripping wet, she peels off a wedge of the fruit and places it in her mouth, biting into this sweet life.

She turns and finds him standing behind her.

Gently, they share another sweet kiss. Much like the first one 50 years before...
only better.

Sonnet for a Lover

When she who has my heart does weep,
I am here to kiss her tears.
With tales of old I give her sleep;
If she permits I will for years.
To hear that her laugh left
Take from me my smile.
Your time of happiness bereft
Will last not but a while.
For you my dear my day is free.
So, come and I shall lend a grin;
And in a moment, you will see
Where hidden yours has been.
Listen now my sweetheart to a kind voice all your own
And never shall you find yourself saddened and alone.

Light Thoughts

Suddenly, I know I will tell you,
How it has become for me.
Light thoughts again--
Floating with you, soft clouds.
Kiss splashes of blue marble,
And rest quietly--
My leg wrapped, holds you near.
Sigh soft and tell you.
Await reaction:
Hopeful, excited, anxious--
Your cool conversation breezes,
Reminding me of the boardwalk,
And the glass apartment.
The sun-soaked maples
And our-sour-apple-cherry-grove.

Poem for a Houseguest

Gone regrettably--
The share of day and night episodes

The kitten-eyed houseguest
Searches with cool, steady lips

In hot, rainy blackness
Quiet blue sheets cast shadows
Expectant of motion

The bedsprings await
The force of coming contractions

A conveyer belt--
Breeze passes empty through the windows

Kitten

At the beach this summer
I was alone with my lover
The young woman I met at school
The one who I'd first seen
In the big lecture hall
Her sex appeal is so enduring
She smells really good
She's not perfumy

I rub up against her
I'm a fluffy kitten
Sometimes very fat
And drowsy and lazy a lot
And she cuddles me up
In her arms and under her chin
With her head moving
From side to side

I adore her petting
And her long sliding grip
Of my muscular henna-red tail
Coiling and relaxing
With the touch of thin fingers
I stretch my back yawning
And hold my eyes closed
And paw gently at the soft mice

Force of Gravity

YOUNG man

P   U   L   L   E   D
                                         O
                                         W
                                         N

by his neck
puts   a LUMP
in one's
throat.

Please Al, don't say so.

Four

"Good, bad, good, good".
A day spent working on herself.
A glorious future lies ahead.
Laws and theorem abound.
Blonde-bob curls forward, defying gentle fingertips.
Drowsy kitten-eyes purr at the page of angles, vectors, forces and
        mass.
Sliding, seemingly, down the incline-- the graphite fist tugs   pulleys
and levers.
Time elapses from zero, and velocity approaches one over none.
Coefficient of friction is nil, but razor kitten-claws dig deep   rows
in the sloped mountainside cornfield.
She will land on four, four, four, four.

Apology

You understand
Emotion-knot I tied

You understand
Kiss-word that I said

You understand
Truth i clashed with pride

You understand
Soft language of my bed

I know
Your nimble-fingers free

I know
Your moist-lipped open ear

I know
Accuse-lie could not be

I know
Pillow-speak my dear

Clown

You whisper your most emphatic statement
I shout my least noteworthy phrase

A carnival of entertaining personalities
Tumbling, and walking on their hands
Swing about the net-less trapeze
Danger and excitement exploding constantly

You are sometimes criticized
The elephant leaves its mark

Safe on the ground, often in the crowd you sit
Applaud and appreciate my skillful and haphazard feats
And I notice a smile amongst all the faces
Unique--impressed and sometimes embarrassed for my foolishness

A circus light at the end of a child's hand
Streaming in an orbit of red light in the darkness of the big top

From a Young Lover Warned

In sheets the shade of surgery gowns
We stretched our bodies long and taught.
And "Give", said Housman, "pounds and crowns"--
Yet not a trinket I have bought.
And oh, how we can operate
While age lies well upon our side.
A score and five she'll celebrate.
My kiss tells what I hide.
The endless rue, the endless rue...
I hope not in our future lies.
So far, this One and Twenty's true...
For we have plenty shared of sighs.
But even Alfred if were right—
The athlete's heart burst young but bright.

Ocean Sonnet

Tomorrow when we meet our lover
North one hundred-fifty turns,
We need not introduce each other;
A lonely mind a lesson learns.
To have you leave, in half I'm torn,
Left only with this pen and sheets.
My days of many names are worn.
A healthy heart one rhythm beats.
The fiber optic waves break short
And crash before the meeting place.
To dance with wolves outside the fort,
Or balance our ballet embrace?
Myself to her the day will bring;
Her kiss for throne if I were king.

Thanksgiving Eve

I am thankful
For the gentle embrace
Of a seemingly sorrowful
World.

Thankful for, family, lover, friend.

I promise the cool, padded palm of mankindness
To the calorous, ruborous, dolorous, tuborous cheek.
Eliminating the stinging slap--
The ferric bite
Of tooth-torn mucosa—
Slowly, postero-sub-pharyngeally.

Primaries

Political profiles outlined in horrific features
Twisted and cork-screwed by the leathery fists
Of a crooked tobacco-stained smile

Slipping in a pile of correctness
They skate smoothly in eights as on ice
Cold saline pulses through circulation

Gestures and motions made meaninglessly
The face of a gargoyle broken to rubble
With age comes the gray of distinct

In the bar-rooms they laugh at the trophies
They turn back the monogrammed sleeves
And a Cuban cigar splits fat fingers

Immunity

To be in
The lone star-state
For the first time
Makes most feel
So small.
Tub ton a
Tnaillirb tnaig that
Sedolpxe, gnidnes
Sregnallahc otni a
Liat nips.
Macrophagically,
Stellate pseudofeet
Extend outward, absorbing
The colding comets of
microcosmic space.
Gorging itself
On the feast of
Crunched numbers,
Prospecti, sickle-eyed
Vaginas, et al.
Specificity
Of presentation
Binds the crowd.
Invaginating--lysing,
Pico-antigens.
Self will
Recognize, and
Protect the
Unharmed survival

Of, self.
Calm splendor,
In the grasp
Of each slide.
Texas man...
G-d.

Quietness

Saddened somewhat
By the inevitable
Coming of nightfall.

That loneliness
One gets as a child
When feeling sorry

For one's self.

The tightly adherent,
Not quite dry kisses
Of the other evening.

One silky garment
devoured by the two
Lovers' quiet melody.

Being Pulled

Forever being pulled -
Being drawn in her direction.

Down the hallway,
Around the corner-
Being pulled.

On days "F" & "G"
I am always wondering
Who, what, where?

My mind, being drawn
Away from the
Here and now.

A limitless force -
Never relenting,
Like gravity.

Pulling me...
Mind, body, soul -
An omnipotent magnetic field.

Her magnificent mouth -
The epicenter of this
Intoxicating power produces

The flash-bulb smile,
The enchanting idiosyncratic movements
Reflecting deep concentration,
The joy-inspiring laughter,
The once in a lifetime kiss.

Forever being pulled -
Always eagerly -
To reconnect.

The Vortex

While I took
My
Shower,

Susan flushed
Her
Mandarin.

Its convulsing
Was
Most regular;

And I sprang
From
The parabolic

Streams of blisteringly
Hot
Spray!

Early Days of Surf

As a wave skims to shore,
I think of you-
Looking as if my movements
Are only at the surface,
Concealing cleverly the undertow
Which pulls at me relentlessly.
Quietly, I cherish thee.
Brief moments
With you: I spent
Comfortably.
And now,
I disregard the rules
Of poetry.
You are much more
Than all the guidelines
Indicate to me,
To the people without hearts
Or brains,
Felt by you in an instant!
Avoiding meddling eyes
Like never
Before.
I thought I would be
Able
To hang up the receiver.
After an hour.
Or was it a minute?
Until you can stay-

For a lifetime
I will come
For you.
I am good

For you.

White Rain

Signs of
How the hot sweat smells of
Sweet corn.

Sunlight
Slips through the tall green leaves
To me.

I roll
In the scorching, loose dirt;
Thinking

Of how
Worthwhile white rain would make
Black mud.

Fred Poured the Drinks

I remember being at a party
Many of them really.
This was in the seventies (TTTTTTT)
and there would always be a stripper
or belly dancer
With a big hunk of glass in her
belly button.
The place would really
howl all night.
We never worried about the neighbors
they were always there
so, they didn't have to complain.
Much better off
throwing your own
bash because you don't
have to drive home ever.
And Fred poured
the drinks
while Al skewered the kabobs
Beef and Lamb
in those days
none of this
chicken and tofu
horse shit.
Place would fill up
with cigarette smoke
real quick
and no one said a fucking word.
Everyone smoked
but of course, it didn't cause cancer
back then.

The Stadium

You leave the stadium although I stay.
A win takes everyone on the team.
Rookies learn from vets how to play.
In the dug-out black coffee curls with white steam.
My uniform muddied and torn in the knees,
The guy I came up with pats clay from his chest.
They struck out the new kid with breaking ball ease
Maybe we'll send him back down for a test.
You can't always blame a player who's green.
Although they threw fat ones all day 'cross the plate.
Not a mark on his cleats, his uniforms' clean
He catches a ride with their club 'cause he's late.
Back at the club house it's gonna be grim.
He better not duck his eyes 'neath his brim.

The Game

I have known not gal just one,
But many as of many kinds.
And they and I have had great fun,
But me she of them not reminds.
They had legs both long and short,
And some were lean, while others round.
I played the game and ruled the sport,
And through one of them I found
A woman who I felt inside without
Touching past her wrist.
He finally turns his jersey in,
For him she is the final win.

Picking Up on An Important Conversation between A Couple of Old Friends, Talking About Things, In A Booth, As I Take the Last Seat at The End Of the Counter at The Luncheonette on Main Street

No?
Yep.
You've godda be kiddin'!
No.
You mean she act-
Yes!...shhh!...yep.
Awe fuck you, come on!
No shit.
Fuck you.
Nope I'm not kidding.
Come on!
What?
Really?
Well, I'm telling you, aren't I?
Wutteryafullashit?
Shut the hell up.
Alright. But I mean sh-
That's it! I shoodinaeventolja.
No, come on, I'll never s-
You better never say anything!
I won't!
Alright. But -
Jesus wuddayathink, thatominasshole or what?
No, but I mean
You're a dick

Look, you have to re-
No... Shit... I mean ... I know. I'm really soh-
Nah. Fergedit. Come on, you ready?
Yeah, let's go.
Leever a nice tip, she was good.
Toobucksanuff?
Yeah.
See you tomorrow, Susan.
Yeah, O.K., Bev.

Second Hand

"Tidth" spits the second hand
Toward
My souring face.

Sand slips steadily
Through
The bombshell's waist.

Bells boom brashly
On
My sore eardrums.

Clock crowds-out
The
Kitchen-coffee cupboards

Dumfounded because
This
Time I doubted

Calypso

No one really knows the measure
Of the ocean's deepest floor.
No one really knows the pleasure
I feel when with her I adore.
Divers swim and subs they dive
Through darkness unsurpassed,
The pressure great but they survive
And Will she be the last?
Or is there yet another cove,
Still one more atmosphere?
I remember when I dove
How far is one light year?
Calypso travelled every sea
Cousteau, Atlantis, Her and Me.

Lemonade

Rain pours like lemonade from a clay pitcher
Crashing to the bottom of a highball glass.
Maybe I am surprised
About the storm.
Some things last so long,
For what reason is it so?
Can't things happen quickly for once around here?
Properly for once!
Rabbit is too fatty.
Everyone loves pizza.
Is that really important right now?
I thought we were talking about something else,
I thought you were talking about someone else.
How did we get off the subject?
Rabbit needs to be trimmed carefully and sliced.
How much is a slice these days?
Always saying something about something,
I think we should make another pitcher.
You don't actually go out and kill those little fellows?
I remember you could get two big slices and a soda.
Forget about that for a second, what were we talking about?
I heard there were barn owls nesting around here.
I guess what I am trying to say might be...
Two cents, can you believe that, you remember that right?
And now Bob with sports, I mean weather, I mean entertainment.
What do you do with the ears after you skin them?
It isn't supposed to taste like chicken!
Toppings were always extra.
How could you pay extra if it only cost two cents to begin with?
I'm not sure.
They may make key chains out of them.

Where the Tune Goes

You have seen rivers run past
Like a wind with no place to go.
The water may forever last
Though the current seems never to slow.
Hard to say where it comes from,
Hard to say why it flows.
Don't know the words then hum
them, see where the tune goes.
From the sky to the mountain,
To the rivers, to sea.
Have you ever had doubt
That here I will be?
The sonnets don't simply exist and drift by,
They begin on a zephyr, from your missing me sigh.

www.ingramcontent.com/pod-product-compliance
Lightning Source LLC
Chambersburg PA
CBHW071915120726
48001CB00005B/1750